GOOD NEWS FOR A BAD NEWS WORLD

Understanding the Gospel

FRAN & JILL SCIACCA

ZondervanPublishingHouse
Grand Rapids, Michigan

A Division of HarperCollinsPublishers

Good News for a Bad News World
Understanding the Gospel
Copyright © 1989, 1992 by Fran and Jill Sciacca
All rights reserved

[Previously published as *Good News for a Bad News World:
Jesus Christ Has a Plan for Your Life*]

Requests for information should be addressed to:
Zondervan Publishing House
Grand Rapids, Michigan 49530

ISBN: 0-310-48061-2

Unless otherwise indicated, Scripture quotations are taken from *The Living Bible*, © 1971, Tyndale House Publishers. Used by permission.

Scripture quotations marked NIV are taken from the HOLY BIBLE: NEW INTERNATIONAL VERSION® (North American Edition). Copyright © 1973, 1978, 1984, by the International Bible Society. Used by permission of Zondervan Publishing House.

"NIV" and "New International Version" are registered in the United States Patent and Trademark Office by the International Bible Society.

All rights reserved. No part of this publication may be reproduced, stored in a retrieval system, or transmitted in any form or by any means—electronic, mechanical, photocopy, recording, or any other—except for brief quotations in printed reviews, without the prior permission of the publisher.

Printed in the United States of America

92 93 94 95 96 / DP / 5 4 3 2 1

Why "Lifelines"?

Who in the world are Fran and Jill ... is it Sky-ocka??

The name "Sciacca" (actually pronounced "Shock-a") is probably not a familiar name to you. Let me take you on a quick trek through our lives so you will know who we are and why we care so much about you.

Fran grew up in the shadow of older identical twin brothers who were football stars. While their photos and accomplishments appeared regularly in newspapers and magazines, Fran found himself wondering who he was besides "the twins' little brother." In high school, he decided to take his talents "elsewhere," completely out of the arena of athletics; he set out to become the best bass guitarist he could be. His rock band was a success, and soon Fran also made it to the pages of the newspaper. On one occasion he played in front of 5,000 people at a "battle of the bands" in Milwaukee, Wisconsin. Fame became Fran's total focus in his search for "self." He was popular at school and was elected class president for three years.

In college, Fran quickly blazed his way to the top of his fraternity. The professional status of his new rock group also gave him personal pride. The band's popularity soared beyond the college campus, and Fran began doing "warm-up" for nationally known entertainers such as Chase and B. J. Thomas. He had finally "arrived" —or so he thought. But why, he wondered, was the feeling of emptiness still lodged so deep in his soul?

Then in one year's time the band began to break up, his girlfriend dumped him, and he received the devastating news that one of his brothers had been seriously wounded in the Vietnam War. It was as if someone had let the air out of his world. He felt alone in the universe. Even his 12 years of religious education in a private school didn't help him.

About this time, God brought a friend into Fran's life who had just committed his own life to Jesus Christ. Late one night in a quiet dorm room, Fran heard from him about the depth of God's love. For the first time, Fran had reason to believe that he was a valuable person, not because he was "cool," or a popular bass guitarist, but because the God of the universe loved him and had paid the penalty for his sin. Fran found the identity he had always longed for in the person of Jesus Christ.

Jill's Journey

I grew up in the "suburbs," graduating with a class of more than 700 students. My years in high school could best be characterized by my quest to know, "Where's the party?" But when I was alone, I often thought about life and death—even suicide. I wrote poems that exposed my inner fears but felt they were "safe" as simple assignments for English class. As best I could, I squelched my spiritual emptiness by dancing, partying, working a little, and playing a lot.

My folly and flippant approach to study in high school forced me to be on probation for the first quarter of college. I buckled down to get good grades but somehow managed to maintain my carefree lifestyle "to the max." I was dating a gifted art student, and together with other friends we embraced the sixties' counterculture. Our philosophy boasted that peace was possible; we could affect society and bring about lasting change. "We" were the answer to all of America's problems.

Yet in two years' time I witnessed the tragic folly of the sixties' philosophy in vivid detail: A best friend from high school had burned out on drugs. Another had died while on drugs. I had seen that our protests against the Vietnam War were leading to prison sentences. People were losing heart. Dropping out. My boyfriend had been committed to a psychiatric ward in a hospital. My best girlfriend, who had entered college on a scholarship, had quit, disillusioned with life. My rock star heroes had fallen from the thrones I'd placed them on. Jimi Hendrix had died. (I had been in the front rows at one of his concerts.) Jim Morrison was gone. Drugs and death seemed to go together. We were not the answer to America's woes—we were part of the problem!

So I fled from the fast lane and started studying philosophy, searching for answers but finding none. Finally, I desperately cried out to the God I had learned about in Sunday school as a child. I had always believed in him but never realized that I could know him personally. Committing my life to him, I made him my Lord and found the peace I hadn't found in all my searching. I joined the ranks of the revival on our college campus, the one that had also swept Fran into the faith. We were radical, but now we had an anchor and a purpose that was really destined to succeed.

And Then, Fran & Jill

We were married after graduation from college. Our first home was in Wisconsin, out in the country, where we attended a small church. There we immediately gravitated to the youth. Three years and one son later, the Lord led us to Denver, Colorado, where Fran went to seminary. While in Denver, we were again drawn to teens as Fran did field work at a local church. Two years and another son later, the Lord led us to Colorado Springs Christian School, where Fran has been teaching Bible in high school ever since! Now we also have the blessed bonus of twin daughters.

We need to tell you all of this for two reasons: First, everything that these studies deal with comes out of our own experience. Second, in many of the things that you're going to look at in *Lifelines: Bible Studies for Students*, we totally "blew it." So not only do we understand the issues at hand, we also know the pain and temptation that go with the territory.

We believe that a genuine relationship with Jesus Christ and with those who are committed to him is the most fulfilling and exciting thing on this sometimes perplexing planet! We're not talking about people who "play church." We're talking about those who are really serious about falling in love with and following the One who died for us.

So be assured that your struggles are familiar to us. They are foes that we have fought too. They are battles that we often lost. But we know there is a way of victory, and we want to help you discover that door of hope.

We pray that, through a personal study of God's Word, you will gain a new vision for a meaningful life, walking with the Lord and living in victory.

Fran and I are a "fun" team. He is the "architect"; I am the "builder." You will find the Bible study section of each chapter designed by Fran. I have helped Fran put a "personal touch" to the studies by telling a story you can relate to, about someone who has been a part of our lives. (Names, gender, and nonessential details have been altered to protect the privacy of those involved.)

There is one more thing we want you to know as you begin this Bible study—we really care about you!

How to Use This Bible Study

This Bible study is part of a series entitled *Lifelines: Bible Studies for Students*. Each study in the series centers around a single issue that you, as a teenager, face in the twentieth century. This study, *Good News for a Bad News World*, carries you into the world of your spiritual life, especially as it relates to what a genuine Christian is and how someone becomes one.

Someone has likened the Christian life to a race. Not a sprint or a relay, but more like a marathon. It lasts a lifetime and takes you over some pretty diverse terrain. *Good News for a Bad News World* can be considered the start of your own personal marathon with God. Its goal is to help you make sure you're on the right track as you pursue a relationship with God.

This study won't answer all the questions you have about God and what it means to know and love him. But it will help you know for sure what a Christian is and whether or not you are one. One of the neatest promises in all of the Bible is found in Jeremiah 29:13: "You will seek me and find me when you seek me with all your heart." (*NIV). God promises that anyone who really wants to get to know him, will. Our prayer for you is that *Good News for a Bad News World* will be the beginning of a long and personally satisfying relationship with the God you read about in the Bible.

Each chapter of *Good News for a Bad News World* includes a real-life story, some personal study questions, and a summary discussion. Look for one major truth, a "Lifeline," as you go through each chapter. If there are specific things the study asks you to do, be sure to do them. The personal insights you pull out of these pages won't help you until you begin to put them into practice.

The only things you will need to complete this study are a Bible, a pen, and an open heart. We suggest that you use the *New International Version* or *The Living Bible*. Make sure that your Bible has both the Old and the New Testaments. We suggest you also have a spiral notebook to record thoughts and ideas that come to you while you study.

If you study *Good News for a Bad News World* in a group, you'll find the optional group discussion questions in each chapter's "Bottom Line" section enlightening and helpful. These questions are deliberately thought-provoking. You'll probably get more out of them if your youth pastor or group leader is present for the discussion.

There is another optional section near the end of each chapter, entitled "His Lines." These are two passages from the Bible that might be helpful as you seek to make the "Lifeline" from that chapter a reality in your own life. You can memorize these verses, put them on your mirror, in your locker, or on the dashboard of your car. Plant them anyplace where they can prompt you to remember the truth when you need it the most.

Other Lifelines

If you enjoy *Good News for a Bad News World*, you may want to try these other *Lifelines* studies:

Are Families Forever?
Strengthening Family Ties

Burgers, Fries & a Friend to Go
Making Friends

Cliques & Clones
Facing Peer Pressure

Does Anyone Else Feel This Way?
Conquering Loneliness and Depression

Is This the Real Thing?
What Love Is and Isn't

So What's Wrong with a Big Nose?
Building Self-Esteem

What Really Matters?
Setting Priorities

1

Who Am I? And Why Am I Here?

Opening Lines

You'd expect that being elected class president for three consecutive years would be enough to provide any high-school student with a sense of purpose and worth. On top of that, add a great girlfriend, a Porsche, a '66 Mustang convertible, and a motorcycle! The only thing I didn't have my senior year in high school was the moon! (Or so it seemed.) But let me share with you a piece of prose that flowed from my inner heart late one evening my last year of high school. It's something that I've given very few people the freedom to read. I willingly share it with you hoping that it will have a lasting impact:

> Each one of us, in our own minds, is the most important. Were our eyes capable of scanning the world and the corridors of time and unveiling the countless billions of humans that have been, are now, and will be, none would compare to ourselves. We live in a sphere that no one can touch.
>
> But stop and think for a minute; are you and I really relevant? Eliminate yourself from life for a few seconds, if

> you can, and let's see exactly what is left. Better yet, what is lost! In all probability, nothing. Your enemies are minus a hindrance. The food that fed you now nourishes someone more deserving and thankful. Your "friends" are saddened, but all humans forget. And the box you're buried in is valued at many times your worth.
>
> Yet somehow in your twisted mind you feel important. You are as insignificant as a leaf in the wind and as an animal you are a failure. If you would stop and think and assess yourself as a whole, I think you would curse the oblivion that bore you and the fools that nurtured you, because in comparison to everything, you are . . . nothing.

In this despondent essay a cry exists that still echoes in my mind: a cry for someone to explain life's meaning to me. The question of life's *purpose* . . . *my* purpose . . . was plaguing me.

There's a bumper sticker that claims, "He who has the most toys when he dies, wins." Is that really all there is to life? Are we to accumulate "toys" and then leave them to someone after us? Was that my destiny too? Or, was there a deeper reason for my being alive? Who *is* man anyway, and why is he around? As a matter of fact, who are *you* anyway, and why are *you* around? I ask this tenderly, but with all sincerity — for until you have an answer to that question, you can't begin to understand what it means to have a relationship with God.

What *is* your answer? Who *are* you?

On the Lines

1. The first two chapters of the Book of Genesis in the Bible contain the account of God's creative work at the beginning of all time. A rather peculiar phrase appears repeatedly in God's description of man in chapter 1, verses 26 and 27, and in chapter 9, verse 6. (A similar phrase occurs in 5:1.) What is that phrase? **(All Bible verses used appear in back of this book.)**

---

2. This phrase basically means that there are things about us as human beings that are *like* God. It doesn't mean that we *are* God, or that we are some sort of "gods." It simply means that in certain ways we are like God.

So if we are all "like God" in some way, do you think it is possible for any of us to find out "who I am" if God isn't somewhere in our explanation? Why not?

___

___

___

3. It appears that *who* I am, and who you are, is very much wrapped up in the fact that we are made in God's "image" or "likeness." But we still need to answer the question of what life is all about. What is man's purpose, the thing for which he was created? The fish were made for water, the birds were made for the air, and they find their purpose in *doing* that for which they were created. But what is *man's* purpose, the reason for which *he* was created? Look up the following verses, and search for the common phrase in each of them:

Jeremiah 9:24

___

Jeremiah 31:34

___

John 17:3

___

From the above verses, what does it appear God wants man to do?

___

What do you think it means to really know someone? Think of your closest friends or perhaps a girlfriend, boyfriend, or family member.

_____

_____

_____

What do you think it means to know *God?*

_____

_____

_____

4. *Why* does God want us to know him? Why does he want us to have a personal relationship with him? Look up the following verses and write out what they have to say as to why God wants us to know him (and him to know us):

John 3:16

_____

Jeremiah 31:3

_____

5. Looking back on what you've covered so far, write, as best you can, answers to the following two questions:

Question #1: Who Am I?

Answer #1: I am . . .

_____

_____

Question #2: What is my purpose for living?

Answer #2: My purpose for living is . . .

Between the Lines

1. Many people are looking for answers to the above two questions. Usually, their answer to, "Who am I?" is based on what they *do*, such as their year in school, their hobbies or athletic accomplishments, and so on. Be honest with yourself right now: if someone had asked you the question, "Who are you?" before you began this study, how would you have answered them?

And how about the second question? Usually our answer to, "What is my purpose?" has to do with what we hope to accomplish in life. How would you have answered the question, "What is my purpose?" before you began this study?

2. Look at your answers above and compare them to the Bible verses — and your answers — in the "On the Lines" section of this study. What have you learned about who *God* says you are, and why you have been given life?

_____

_____

Closing Lines

As do most seniors, I eventually graduated from high school and moved on to college. The funny thing was that those two questions, "Who am I?" and, "Why am I alive?" graduated with me and followed me to college, still hunting and haunting me. It took me until the spring of my sophomore year in college to come to the conclusions that I trust you have come to just from completing this chapter.

And the sad thing is, I suffered much damage and pain from not having good answers to those questions. You see, just like a fish out of water, or an eagle on the ground, a human being who has no relationship with his or her God is a miserable thing. The tragedy is that, in our attempt to *find* our identity and purpose, we usually get involved in all the wrong things. I did. Choosing to live for myself, without a real purpose, had a high price tag. I hurt others and I hurt myself.

So if our identity and purpose comes from knowing God, why do so few people seem to know him? And why do many who *want* to find God seem to be looking "in all the wrong places"? The next two chapters will deal with those questions. (P.S. Things are going to get worse in this study before they get better, so please hang in there!)

Lifeline

I am made in God's image, and he wants me to know him.

His Lines

Genesis 1:27

John 17:3

The Bottom Line (For Group Discussion)

1. Carl Sagan has said that the "Cosmos is all there is, was, and ever will be." [Carl Sagan, *Cosmos* (New York: Random House, 1980), 4.] If Sagan is right and there is no God, can people really find answers to the two big questions we discussed in this chapter? Why or why not?

2. The theory of evolution has been accurately diagrammed as :

All of life = impersonal matter + time + chance

Do you see any problems with this explanation for who man is and why he's around? Explain.

3. Today everyone seems to be demanding their "rights" — like gay rights, children's rights, and women's rights, to name just a few. Based on our study so far, why do human beings have a feeling that they're important? Do you think most people really *understand* where this feeling of worth comes from? Explain.

4. We noted that many people, in their search for a purpose in life, get involved in things that are destructive and harmful. Do you agree that this is true? Why or why not?

2
I Feel Guilty

Opening Lines

Jill had gone to church most of her life. She had heard plenty about Jesus Christ and believed that he had died on the cross for the sins of mankind. She had been baptized as an infant and confirmed when she was in junior high. Hence, she was a church member in good standing, even though her attendance had sharply declined during her teen years.

Jill would have fit the standard American definition of "Christian." That's why what happened to her is so significant.

Throughout childhood and on into high school, Jill drifted off to sleep each night presenting the same plea upward: "Lord, please forgive me of my sins." She ended each day with a frustrating sense of guilt about the life she was living. This habit of asking daily for God's forgiveness was carried on into college. It was like possessing a secure savings account. Jill wanted to know that her "account" balanced out each night. And if asking for God's forgiveness seemed necessary in high school, it was absolutely critical in college, for Jill's lifestyle quickly took a turn for the worse. The party scene could count on Jill's presence. She was fond of having a good time.

Yet, beneath the surface, Jill was on a frantic search for the very thing we looked at in chapter 1 — a lasting reason to live. Jill was watching the new Christians on campus (I was one of them!) and wondering why they were so happy. Jill *wasn't* happy.

But Jill was a Christian . . . wasn't she?

One of the new believers (a girl who used to go to the bars with Jill) had given her a Bible. She read it periodically before bed, sincerely seeking to understand its message. But, to her dismay, the more she read, the less she could understand. The more she prayed, the more she was convinced that her prayers weren't passing beyond the walls of her dingy apartment.

What was wrong, anyway? If we humans were made to know God and have a relationship with him, then why wasn't it working? What was it that kept Jill from "breaking through" to God? Why did she fearfully ask for God's forgiveness each night, while wondering where she would spend eternity if she died before morning? As a matter of fact, if *you* died tonight, do you know where you would spend eternity?

On the Lines

1. Let's go back to "the beginning" again. Turn to Genesis 2:15-17 and 3:1-7. This is called the "Fall of Man." When Adam and Eve chose to disobey God, they became responsible for something very terrible. Look at Romans 5:12. What does this verse say were the results of Adam's sin?

_____

_____

2. Who has been affected by sin, according to Romans 3:23?

_____

3. Let's take a look at just what sin has done to mankind. Below is a list of Bible references and across from them is a list of statements. Connect with a line the reference and the statement it matches.

BIBLE REFERENCE	THE EFFECT OF SIN
Romans 6:23	Sin separates me from God
Hebrews 9:27	Sin affects my relationships with others
James 4:1-2	Sin results in death
Isaiah 59:1-2	Sin leads to judgment

4. Look up Romans 7:14-20. Read it slowly and carefully. Does it seem from this passage that sin is simply something we *do,* or is it something more serious, like a part of us? Explain your answer.

_____

_____

_____

_____

5. Write out everything you've learned so far about what sin is, and what it does. In your answer be personal — write about yourself. Use words like "me" and "I," not words such as "us" and "we."

_____

_____

_____

_____

_____

Between the Lines

1. Write out below the things you see in your life that support the fact that sin is a *part* of you, not just things you do that are wrong. (*Example:* I try not to lie to my parents, but I'm afraid of being punished, so I keep lying.)

_____

_____

_____

_____

2. It has been said that there is only one "throne" in each person's heart. And only one of two people can sit on that throne: God . . . or that person. Sin is the result of *us* deciding that *we* will sit on our throne and rule our lives. It means that *we* will decide what we will do, who we will be, what is wrong and right. It means that we will do what we want with our lives. I want you to be totally honest right now. Who sits on the throne of *your* life?

☐ God ☐ me ☐ I'm not sure

3. Let's go back to that sobering question at the end of the "Opening Lines" section. If for some reason you *did* die before the sun set today, do you know where you would spend eternity?

☐ I don't know ☐ Heaven ☐ Hell

Closing Lines

So, why *couldn't* Jill break through to God? If man's purpose is to know God and have a personal relationship with him, then why was Jill feeling so guilty and so distant from God? She believed the Bible was the Word of God, and she even tried to understand it.

The verse you looked up in Isaiah says clearly why Jill couldn't find God:

> Surely the arm of the Lord is not too short to save, nor his ear too dull to hear. But your *iniquities* have separated you from your God; your sins have hidden his face from you, so that he will not hear.
>
> (Isaiah 59:1-2, NIV, italics added)

The reason Jill was feeling so guilty is quite clear: she *was* guilty! The reason Jill felt that God was so far away from her is because he was! Even though man is made to have a personal relationship with the God in whose image he was made, he *can't!* And worst of all, it's not God's fault, it's ours. Ever since Adam committed the first sin, all human beings have been sinners by nature, and our sin separates us from God. In fact, *you* are a sinner too and *your* sin separates you from God.

If you feel guilty and far away from God, there's a good reason for that — it's true. That's the bad news. Or perhaps you don't *feel* guilty, but you do know that there is a great gulf between you and God. Such a conclusion is correct.

If this were the last chapter in this Bible study, you'd have good reason for feeling the way you did in the first chapter — helpless and hopeless.

But this isn't the last chapter! And there's *good news* coming. . . . But can you take some more bad news first?

Lifeline

The bad news is: My sin separates me from God.

His Lines

Romans 5:12

Romans 6:23

The Bottom Line (For Group Discussion)

1. Do I sin because I am a sinner, or am I sinner because I sin? Explain.

2. Are there "degrees" of sin in God's eyes? Are some sins more serious than others? Explain.

3. Are there degrees of sin as far as *consequences* are concerned? Explain.

4. Does the fact that all people are sinners do away with the idea that some people are "better" than others? Why or why not?

5. Some people say that a loving God could never send anyone to hell. Do you think that a just and holy God could ever send a sinner to heaven? Explain. (*Note:* Saying God can do anything he wants is *not* a valid answer. God cannot do anything that is contrary to his nature.)

3
Enough Is Never Enough

Opening Lines

I'd like you to join me on an imaginary journey. We are in a room about the size of, say . . . your own bedroom. You and I are invisible spectators of something very unusual. The room is completely empty. No furniture, no posters, no color, no sound. It is so silent that it's almost spooky. Then, in one corner of the room, we see the hazy, ghost-like reflection of an elderly woman. Her face is aglow with gladness; she hums softly to herself while knitting a pair of booties for her grandchild.

A snarling noise draws our attention to the opposite corner, where crouches the repulsive-looking ghost of a violent old man. He is cursing under his breath. His jaw is locked and his teeth are clenched. He babbles something about hating his only brother and wanting to steal his inheritance.

Suddenly, the small room becomes completely dark. Only our memory will possess the places where we are standing. The darkness seems to have substance; we can almost feel it. Then, without warning, we hear a voice calling us: "Watch carefully," the voice announces. "I am about to let you see into the very *souls* of these two people."

We shudder and try to turn away, but the voice continues: "I will reveal to you the contents of their hearts — by means of *light*.

I will cause the goodness in each of them to become like light. The greater their goodness, the brighter their light will be."

While we stand expectantly in the darkness, a very faint flicker of light appears in the corner where the crude man crouches. If it hadn't been so totally dark in the room, we might not have even noticed it. Then, as quickly as it appeared, the light vanishes.

Across the room, in the kind old woman's corner, another light appears. It grows and grows until it illuminates the room with blinding light. It turns to contrasting colors, beautiful to behold.

This "performance" of lights repeats three or four times — first the dim glow from the hateful old man, then the bright flood of light showing the goodness of the gentle grandmother. Then, as quickly as the whole adventure began, it ends.

Pretty strange, huh? But think about it: Isn't this a good illustration of the way you and I tend to view people? Don't we see some people as being "better" or having more "goodness" than others? If we *were* able to see into people's hearts the way we did in this fantasy, wouldn't we see big differences? I mean, aren't some people just better than others? And if that's true, isn't God going to be more inclined to like the *good* people? Doesn't it seem logical that good people will go to heaven and bad people will go to hell? If *you* were God, isn't that how you would handle it?

On the Lines

1. Look up the verses below and note the things "good" people might try to *do* to win God's favor. Then, write down what the verse says about whether that activity will, in fact, help them *earn* a relationship with God:

BIBLE VERSE	THE ACTIVITY	EARN RELATIONSHIP WITH GOD?
Ephesians 2:8-9	_____	☐ yes ☐ no
John 5:39-40	_____	☐ yes ☐ no

Romans 3:20 _____ ☐ yes ☐ no

Matthew 7:22-23 _____ ☐ yes ☐ no

In summary, can people do anything, on their own, to gain a relationship with God?

☐ yes   ☐ no

2. This is discouraging, isn't it? Man is totally powerless to do anything about being separated from God because of sin. But, *why* can't he do anything? Isn't "being good" enough? What does God expect from us, anyway?

To answer this very important question, let's look first at Psalm 11:7. What word describes God? (Use the *New International Version,* or check in the back of this book.)

_____

Now look at Romans 3:10. What does it say that man *isn't?*

_____

Finally, look at the first part of Romans 3:20. What does it say that man needs to be "declared" to have a relationship with God?

_____

3. If God's standard isn't "goodness," then what is his standard for accepting us into a relationship with him?

_____

(We will talk about this word again in the "Closing Lines" section below.)

4. Looking back over the past two chapters and this one, write out below as best you can what you understand so far:

My understanding of who man is:

_____

_____

_____

_____

My understanding of how God feels about man:

_____

_____

_____

_____

My understanding of what God wants for man:

_____

_____

_____

_____

My understanding of what man's trouble is:

_____

_____

_____

_____

Between the Lines

1. There's a bumper sticker you may have seen that says, "Life Is So Much Easier Since I Gave Up Hope!" Some people seek to deal with the two basic questions of chapter 1 — "Who am I?" and "What is my purpose for living?" — by simply giving up all hope of finding an answer! They try to go through life ignoring God, and ignoring the fact that they are made for a relationship with him. Sometimes they run from God; sometimes they simply fill their lives with so much activity and people that the noise drowns out the haunting questions.

Have you been doing that? I mean, have you tried to hold God at arm's length, or run away from him completely? If so, then today is the time to get serious. Why don't you stop right now, and tell God that you realize what you've been doing and that you want to learn how to begin a relationship with him? Pray right where you are, right now. . . .

2. Or maybe you've been a religious "good guy" all your life. You've gone to church, maybe even taught Sunday school or led your church's youth group. And now you realize that you've been assuming that all your "goodness" will merit a relationship with God — but you've come to see that it won't! Now is the time for you to admit that to God. Tell him you want to know how to become a real Christian, someone who has a genuine relationship with him. Stop and pray right now. . . .

3. Or, maybe you were born into a Christian home and have just assumed that you've been accepted by God on the "group plan"! I've got sobering news: Being born in a Christian home doesn't make you a Christian any more than being born in an oven will make you a biscuit! *You* need to stop right now too. Ask God to make the rest of this Bible study as real to you as the front of your hand. Tell him that you want to know exactly what a Christian is, and how to become one.

Closing Lines

There *were* obvious differences between the grandmother and the old man in the "Opening Lines" section. One really *was* a better person than the other. And you and I can see those kinds of differences between people. We can even compare our *own* goodness with what we see in the lives of those around us. Often our conclusion is that *we* aren't as bad as "so-and-so."

But, God's standard is not goodness vs. badness. His standard is *righteousness* — the word that's used to describe him in Psalm 11:7. Let me define righteousness by an example: If we took the lights of the grandmother and the old man and held them side-by-side up against the sun, *both* lights would be lost in the sun's blaze. The same is true of our *goodness* compared to God's *righteousness:* no human being's goodness can measure up to God's *total* goodness, or *righteousness* . . . even though that person's goodness may be much greater than the goodness of other human beings.

To use another example with which you are probably familiar, God does not grade on a curve. It's a Pass/Fail system with him. You are either 100 percent righteous or you are not righteous at all. Mere goodness doesn't count.

It's pretty obvious, isn't it, that *no one* passes under this system? Everyone is condemned, because no one is righteous except God. That, my friend, is the last of the bad news. What we need now is some *good* news! Do you know what the Greek word for good news is? It's the word we translate *gospel*. And that's what you're going to hear about now. See ya next chapter!

Lifeline

Still more bad news: There's nothing *I* can do to be righteous in God's sight.

His Lines

Romans 3:20

Ephesians 2:8-9

The Bottom Line (For Group Discussion)

1. Is it right for God to send anyone to hell? Explain.

2. What about those who have never heard of Christianity?

3. Why is it that some people don't seem to feel a need for salvation? (See Luke 18:11 for a clue.)

4. Listen to Steve Camp's song, "I'm a Stranger to Your Holiness," on his album, *Whatever You Ask* (Sparrow Records) and discuss its message.

5. Does God's standard of righteousness make salvation and eternal life *more* available, or *less* available? Explain.

4
The Painless Paddling

Opening Lines

Grant was one of those guys who will probably be late for his own funeral. He was never on time for his first-period class. Day after day, the sound of the bell entered Mr. Kenston's U.S. History class ahead of Grant.

Finally, Mr. Kenston could take it no more. He hauled Grant off to the headmaster's office and laid out the charges: "Late to first hour ten times in ten days!" The headmaster stared sternly at Grant and said, "Young man, if you are tardy to first hour one more time, I will have no option but to paddle you!" Giving swats to an eighth-grader was not normal procedure, but Grant had defied every other form of punishment.

The next day, the stage was set. The clock was the judge as it ticked toward 8:25. On schedule, the bell rang . . . but Grant was not present in U.S. History.

About five minutes later, guess who walked in? Yup, good ol' Grant. And he was wearing a grin as wide as a garage door! Mr. Kenston politely excused himself from the class, firmly grasped Grant by his right elbow, and escorted him to the headmaster's office.

There, a battle of wills was fought. The headmaster began, "Grant, you have flagrantly disobeyed my authority. I told you yesterday what would happen if you were late today. I am forced to paddle you."

Grant's reply was abrupt and rebellious: "You ain't paddling me! *No one's* going to paddle *me!*" The two shouted back and forth a few more times before Mr. Kenston finally asked the headmaster if he could speak to him privately in the hall.

In the hallway that morning an incredible event took place. But we'll get to that in the "Closing Lines" section. (Don't read ahead!) Meanwhile, a defiant young man who deserved to be paddled sat in the headmaster's office, plotting his escape. He had shown a total disrespect for authority, aware that punishment would be the result.

But Grant's dilemma is really no different than yours or mine. As we learned in the last two chapters, we stand guilty before a righteous God. We have no valid excuses for our sins. We *deserve* the consequences — separation from God, judgment, and even death.

Some of our sins are obvious and known by all. Others are secret sins that have their home in our thought life — sins like anger and jealousy, greed and lust. But in God's system of justice, *sin* is *sin.* We can hide nothing from him. David said, "O Lord, you have examined my heart and know everything about me. You know when I sit or stand. When far away you know my every thought" (Psalm 139:1-2).

None of us can claim that our conscience is clear. We are all condemned.

It seems pretty hopeless, doesn't it? If God is to be consistent, he should send you and me both to hell. Is there any possible way that God can execute justice and still be merciful and loving? I mean, is there any conceivable way for our sin to be justly punished and for us to come out of it alive?

Do you realize that your eternal destiny hangs on whether you answer yes or no to that question? So, what will it be?

On the Lines

1. According to the previous chapters, these are the main problems you are facing right now because of your sin:

1. You are separated from God.

The Painless Paddling

2. You are destined to die and then to face God's holy judgment.

Let's take a very close look at some Bible verses and see what they have to say about these two problems. Look at each verse and answer these questions:

Who is this verse speaking of?

What does it say about:
　　our separation from God?
　　our eternal destiny?

Verse: 1 Peter 3:18

Who?

_____

What does it say?

_____

_____

_____

Verse: John 1:29

Who:

_____

What does it say?

_____

_____

_____

Verse: Romans 5:6

Who?

_____

What does it say?

_____

_____

_____

_____

Verse: 2 Corinthians 5:21 (The "him" in this verse refers to Jesus.)

Who?

_____

What does it say?

_____

_____

_____

_____

2. A verse that really summarizes what all these verses are saying is 1 Timothy 2:3-6a:

> This is good and pleases God our Savior, for he longs for all to be saved and to understand this truth: *That God is on one side and all the people on the other side, and Christ Jesus, himself man, is between them to bring them together, by giving his life for all mankind.*

The Painless Paddling

3. This verse could be illustrated as follows:

4. In the space below, write out what you believe is the main point of all the verses you've looked at in this chapter.

_____

_____

_____

_____

_____

_____

Between the Lines

1. Look at the diagram in question 3 above. Draw a small stick figure on that diagram that represents where *you* are in your relationship with God at this moment. Are you on the side of *man*? The side of *God*? Or do you not know *which* side you are on? Think carefully. Answer honestly.

2. If you find yourself on the side of man, are you thinking that the things that you've done are so bad that God can't forgive you? If you're feeling this way, look up 1 Timothy 1:15-16. Paul had openly opposed Christians and even sentenced them to death before his own conversion. He makes a very startling statement here about sinful people. What is it?

_____

_____

Matthew 9:13 records the words of Jesus himself on this subject. What does he say?

_____

_____

3. If you placed your stick figure on the side of man, then you will want to take the next chapter very seriously. If you placed it on the side of God, you may want to move on to chapter 6.

Closing Lines

Did you jump ahead to see what happened to Grant? I don't blame you. It's an awesome story.

We left Grant in the headmaster's office waiting for a paddling — the punishment prescribed for his habitual tardiness. And a paddling was given that day in punishment for that offense. And it was a *severe* paddling, too. I mean we're talking about the type that makes you wonder if your backside will glow in the dark!

The unbelievable thing is that Grant didn't get paddled —

Mr. Kenston did!

No, you didn't read this wrong: Mr. Kenston was paddled by the headmaster that day. And, like I said, it was a severe paddling. Why? Well, during their powwow in the hallway Mr. Kenston told the headmaster that he really thought Grant needed to learn something more than obedience to authority. He felt that Grant needed to experience in an unforgettable way that Jesus Christ took the punishment that rightfully belonged to him. Mr. Kenston decided that the most graphic way to communicate the good news of the gospel to Grant was for him to take the punishment Grant deserved, just like Christ, on the Cross, took the punishment for the sins of all mankind.

So, Grant got to watch as the headmaster pounded that paddle against the backside of *his teacher* instead of him! Then, without a word, Mr. Kenston walked out of that office, and the headmaster sat down beside a rebellious but stunned young man and told him how Jesus Christ had taken the punishment he deserved for his sins; he told him how Christ's love made him willing to die so that Grant might go free.

Powerful, huh? But, do you know something even more profound? It's true for you and me too! Jesus Christ, the sinless son of God, took upon himself the punishment that you and I deserve. And in so doing, God was able to be just (because punishment was carried out) and loving and merciful (because you and I were not condemned). Now that's good news, isn't it?

Lifeline

The good news is: Jesus Christ took the punishment I deserve.

His Lines

1 Peter 3:18

2 Corinthians 5:21

The Bottom Line (For Group Discussion)

1. Listen to "Clean Before My Lord," by Petra on their *Beat the System* album, and "He Covers Me," by Steve Camp on his *One-on-One* album. Discuss how the message of these two songs relates to this chapter.

2. Some have said that salvation is "cheap" because there is nothing that man can do, and that God has done it all. Do you agree? Why, or why not?

3. Look at Romans 5:8 as a group. Does that verse have more meaning to you now that you've finished this chapter? Explain.

4. Many Christians seem to be proud and arrogant. Does that seem right, based on how they were able to become Christians in the first place? Explain.

5
Take It or Leave It

Opening Lines

In the early spring of my second year of college, my whole life cratered. I found myself harassed and hounded by the basic questions you studied in the first chapter. Was there a purpose for me on this planet? Did God exist? Could I know him? My well-established career plans had totally evaporated when my twin brothers changed theirs — the three of us had been planning to be partners in an optometry practice.

Another blow came when my girlfriend back home decided that long distance relationships were not her style. I found myself totally alone. I was aching inside.

But during this dismal time a couple of guys had been regularly drifting into my dorm room. They shared the same message with me that you have discovered in the first four chapters: God loved me and had a purpose for my life; but my own sin was preventing me from making it happen. They told me — or at least *tried* to tell me — that Jesus Christ had paid the penalty for my sin, and that the way to God was opened to me through his sacrifice on the cross. I listened, but wasn't interested . . . yet.

Finally, after a few more family tragedies and a total loss of direction for my own life, I found myself desperate, almost suicidal.

There was one particular guy on my dorm floor whom I really liked. His name was Wally Schultz. I knew that Wally had become a Christian that quarter, but I sensed that his friendship towards me was sincere — he wasn't just concerned about "converting" me. That's why, about 3:00 one April morning in 1970, when I was feeling totally hopeless, I felt the freedom to knock on Wally's door.

Wally unlatched the door, stood there, and before he could think about whether or not to welcome me in at that awful hour, I blurted out, "Wally, I don't know what to do with my life!"

Wally invited me in and we began to talk. I wanted to know why life was worth living. But his first question caught me totally off guard. "Fran," he asked, "are you a Christian?"

I thought to myself, "Oh great, my life's crumbling all around me and this guy wants me to talk about God!" I fired back a rigid response, "Of course I'm a Christian! I've been baptized, confirmed, and I spent twelve years in a parochial school." I figured he would back off when he discovered how much I knew about God. But, he didn't!

In fact, he asked me two more questions that literally left me breathless. The first one was simple. "Fran, what do you believe about Jesus Christ?"

That's easy, I thought. I proceeded to rattle off the standard stuff I had learned in confirmation class at church.

But Wally was digging deeper. "Do you really *believe* all that, Fran?" he asked. I assured him that I did. Then he cornered me with a stinging question: "If you really believe all those things, Fran, how does your belief differ from Satan's? He believes all that stuff too, because it's true and he *knows* it's true."

I was stunned! I had a reputation around campus for my quick wit — I played in a band, and could hold a crowd in the palm of my hand with my winsome words. But now I couldn't even convince one guy that I knew what he was talking about. He had shown me exactly what my twelve years of religious education had done for me . . . it had educated me! I knew a lot *about* God, but it was now convincingly clear that I didn't *know* God.

As the sad truth sank in, I slowly dropped down on the bed and fixed my gaze on the floor. Wally proceeded to tell me all the things that you've discovered in the first four chapters of this study. That early April morning, as Wally walked with me from death to life, he took me page by page through a booklet that has been reproduced for you on pages 63-70 of this study.

One particular verse that Wally read to me brought all my fuzzy thoughts suddenly into focus:

> And what is it that God has said? That he has given us eternal life, and that this life is in his Son. So whoever has God's Son has life; whoever does not have his Son, does not have life.

(1 John 5:11-12)

Finally, Wally faced me and looked me squarely in the eyes. "Fran," he asked, "do you have Jesus Christ?" I knew that I didn't, but how was I supposed to "get" Jesus Christ? How does someone come to possess the son of God? Do you know? As a matter of fact, do you *have* Jesus Christ in *your* life right now?

On the Lines

1. First of all, let's look at some Bible verses that explain a little more about what it means to *have* the son of God. Look up Galatians 2:20. Paul is speaking here of a Christian. What does he say about Jesus Christ here?

_____

_____

_____

Look at Ephesians 3:17. What does this verse say about *where* Christ dwells and how he gets there?

_____

_____

_____

2. We need to understand a little better just what our *hearts* are in order to comprehend what it means to have Christ living in our hearts. Look up Proverbs 4:23. A "wellspring" is the source of water for a well. If the wellspring is contaminated, the whole well is ruined. If it is pure, the well is pure. What does this verse seem to be teaching about what your heart is?

_____

_____

_____

3. Try to summarize what you understand so far about what it means to *have* Jesus Christ.

_____

_____

_____

_____

4. So *how* does someone "get" Jesus Christ. Remembering that "he who has God's Son has life," we can answer that question from the following verses, which tell how we receive eternal life:

Romans 6:23

_____

Ephesians 2:8

_____

5. God uses the picture of a "gift" for salvation. When someone is giving a gift, both the giver and the receiver have a responsibility, if everything is going to happen as intended. What is the responsibility of the giver?

_____

What is the responsibility of the receiver?

_____

6. If salvation is a gift of God — he is the giver and man is the receiver — then what is *man's* responsibility regarding that gift?

_____

_____

_____

Between the Lines

1. According to the verse Wally shared with me in that dorm room, a person either "has" or "has not" the son of God. Jesus Christ and the gift of forgiveness are either yours or they're not. As you reflect on this chapter so far, and you look back to the illustration on page 35, which phrase best describes you right now? Check the boxes that apply:

☐ I do *not* have Jesus Christ.

☐ I have *received* God's gift of salvation.

☐ I have *not* received God's gift of salvation.

☐ I *do* have Jesus Christ.

☐ I *want* to have Jesus Christ.

2. If you checked the first, third, or fifth box above, then you need to ask yourself one more question: "Is there any reason why

I wouldn't want to receive God's gift of salvation right now?" If you realize that you do *not* have Jesus Christ, and therefore are *not* a child of God, and you want to make *today* the day that you receive God's gracious gift of forgiveness and salvation, then you can! It's a matter of faith. And faith is trusting that what God says is true, that's all it is! You can exercise faith by praying the following prayer:

> God, I realize that you love me and that you have a specific purpose for my life: to know and love you. I also have come to realize and accept the fact that I am a sinner and justly deserve your judgment and punishment. But, your Word says that your only Son, Jesus Christ, died in my place and paid the penalty that I deserve for my sins. As a result, you offer me forgiveness for my sins as a gift that I cannot earn and do not deserve.
>
> Lord, today I want to accept that free gift of salvation and ask that your Son, Jesus Christ, take control of my heart — that part of me that controls my whole life. Last of all, in faith I believe that you can be trusted, that all of this is true, and that *right now* I am a Christian, totally forgiven and a child of yours forever! Thank you, God.

3. If you prayed the above prayer and accepted God's gift of salvation, then fill in the commitment statement below:

> **"I, _____, on the _____ of _____, 19___, accepted God's gift of eternal life and am now a Christian, a child of God."**

4. Tell at least two people about your decision.

Closing Lines

In that dorm room more than eighteen years ago, Wally Schultz (a recent convert himself!) told me something very profound. He said that salvation was a free gift; there was *nothing* I could do to earn it.

Wally used another helpful comparison as well. He told me that, because of my sin, I was really living in the sealed quarters of a prison cell; I was condemned and awaiting my execution. But then, the prison warden appeared and said, "Fran, you've been granted a pardon by the governor. He alone possessed the power to release you — and he has. You are free to go."

But as Wally also pointed out, even though I was pardoned, it was still up to me to get up and walk out of that prison cell! Forgiveness is indeed a gift, but gifts are of no value unless they are *accepted*. Salvation is a gift, eternal life is a gift, and becoming God's child is a gift. But I needed to reach out to God in faith, and *take that gift!*

Well, about four o'clock in the morning that April day, Fran Sciacca walked out of Wally's room and went outside. Alone, he stood and prayed a prayer almost identical to the one printed above. Now, nearly twenty years later, I'm passing along to you the things that Wally shared with me that night — the Good News that changed my life forever. My prayer is that you will let it change your life forever too. Will you?

Lifeline

Salvation is a gift, but I must accept it.

His Lines

Romans 6:23

John 5:24

The Bottom Line (For Group Discussion)

1. Two people had appointments on the hundredth floor of an office building. One of them stood for hours in front of the elevator, saying over and over that he truly believed the elevator could take him to the hundredth floor. The other one simply stepped into the elevator and pushed the button marked "100." Did both of these people have faith in the elevator? Explain.

2. Why can't God just make everyone his child, without their accepting the gift of forgiveness?

3. There are different reasons why things are free. One of them is because they're cheap and worthless. But, why do you think salvation is free?

4. Does a "free" salvation make you want to "repay" God for his kindness, or live a reckless life? Explain.

5. Some tend to look at salvation merely as "Fire Insurance." What do you think they mean by that phrase? Explain.

6
Paid in Full

Opening Lines

Teaching in a Christian school constantly provides me with surprises. This is especially true when we have prayer time each Monday. Often, I am not prepared for what I hear as students share prayer requests. The requests are usually from what I call the "safe zones" — areas of life that aren't *too* personal. This could be problems with parents, relatives, friendships, or work. But Tony's request was really different.

Tony was an outgoing and positive junior, whose enthusiasm was electric. He encouraged the entire class just by his attitude. Consequently, when upbeat Tony raised his hand I wasn't prepared for what I was about to hear. He requested prayer for some friends of his family. It seems that the son and daughter-in-law of these friends had been traveling with their eight-month-old son. Their car was hit head-on by a drunk driver. The son and daughter-in-law were killed instantly, though the baby somehow survived the crash.

The parents of the young father were understandably devastated by the news. In a moment's madness, they had lost their son and daughter-in-law. As Tony said, "They are really hurting right now. They've asked everyone they know to pray for them."

So far, the request seemed very normal. But Tony's next

words made my heart cringe as I pondered the consequences. "They'd also appreciate prayer because the dad is going to the jail to talk to the drunk driver who killed his son and daughter-in-law. He wants to share the gospel with him."

I couldn't believe my ears! How could this broken-hearted father walk into a jail cell and share God's love and forgiveness with the very man who had killed two members of his family? When I tried to imagine myself in that father's place, I could think of nothing but anger and revenge. What if it had been my Ben or Geoff? Forgiveness is one thing, but this? And so soon? What would have gone through *your* mind if you had been sitting in my classroom that morning? Would you have condemned the careless driver?

On the Lines

1. In the last chapter, you discovered that salvation is a free gift — there's nothing you can do to earn it. Hopefully, you made a decision to *accept* God's gift of forgiveness. But how long is salvation good for? I mean, can't you lose it just as quickly as you got it? Let's take a look at some verses that address this question. Look each of them up, and write out what you think it is saying about how *secure* your forgiveness is:

John 10:27-29

_____

_____

_____

Romans 8:39-40

_____

_____

_____

Paid in Full

2. Write out two things that you believe could *separate* you from God:

1. _____

2. _____

Now go back and read Romans 8:39-40 again. According to that verse, can either of your two items separate you from God?

☐ yes ☐ no

3. Sometimes, we *feel* that we've done things that could separate us from God. In other words, our own *hearts* condemn us. What does 1 John 3:19-20 say about this?

_____

_____

_____

4. There's really only one person who could condemn you, the one you sinned against in the first place — God. First of all, write out what you believe the word "condemn" means (use a dictionary if you want to):

_____

_____

Now, look up the following verses and write out what they have to say about being condemned:

Romans 8:1

_____

John 5:24

_____

John 3:18

_____

5. Let's take this a step further. Imagine that you are in a courtroom. In the courtroom with you is the judge, the attorney defending you, and the attorney prosecuting you. Who do you think the prosecuting attorney would be? (*Hint:* It has to be someone who can bring *legitimate* charges against you.)

☐ you ☐ Jesus Christ ☐ God the Father

Look at Psalm 9:7-8. According to this verse, who is the judge?

☐ you ☐ Jesus Christ ☐ God the Father

Look at Romans 8:34. Who is your defending attorney?

☐ you ☐ Jesus Christ ☐ God the Father

Finally, look at Romans 8:31. What does this verse have to say about how secure your forgiveness is?

_____

_____

_____

6. Summarize what you've learned so far about your security as a Christian.

_____

_____

_____

_____

_____

7. Even though your relationship with God as his child is secure, that does not mean that you can sin freely. Your sins are still a serious matter, and they have an effect on your relationship with God — just as your behavior has an effect on your relationship with your earthly parents. Look at 1 John 1:9 and Proverbs 28:13. What do these two verses have to say about sin?

_____

_____

_____

_____

Between the Lines

1. The thing you need most as a new Christian is some sort of spiritual food. God's Word, the Bible, is the Christian's primary source of nourishment. If you don't have one, you can use the "dollar-off" coupon in the back of this book to get a copy of *The Everyday New Testament* at your local Christian bookstore (or from World Wide Publications). It contains some helpful articles by Billy Graham, introductions and study guides for all the New Testament books, and a convenient Bible dictionary.

2. Locate the Gospel of John near the front of the New Testament, and read one chapter each day. You will probably want to have a notebook handy to write down thoughts and questions that come to mind as you read. Be especially attentive for new insights about Jesus himself, and also look for ways in which you are *like* or *unlike* the people Jesus encounters.

3. Also, now that you are a member of God's "family," you'll want to start spending time with other Christians. Try to find a good church that teaches the Bible *and* has a good youth program — so that you'll be able to meet other Christians your age. Make a commitment to attend Sunday school regularly for at least one month.

4. Finally, *Some Assembly Required,* another Bible study in the *Lifelines: Getting a Hold on Life* series is designed to take you deeper as you begin your new life as a Christian. Get a copy from your local Christian bookstore, or write and ask for *Some Assembly Required* from:

> Grason Company
> P.O. Box 1240
> Minneapolis, MN 55440

Closing Lines

If Tony's amazing story about the forgiving father made my mind reel — wondering what I would have done — then his story three days later pushed me over the edge!

The father whose son and daughter-in-law were killed *did* in fact go visit the drunk driver who had hit them. Not only did he visit the man, but he told him that he forgave him for killing his children. He went on to explain that God also forgave him, because of the death of Jesus Christ for his sins. Even the sin of drunk driving. He told the man that God wanted him to accept this forgiveness and commit his life to Jesus Christ.

What do you think happened? The man became a Christian! I'm serious. He really did.

Does this story bother you? I mean, have you been putting yourself into the story and saying things like, "I would never forgive that guy!" or "I hope he goes to prison for life!"

Think of it this way: There were mainly two people who were in a position to either forgive the drunk driver or hate him. And they were the parents of the two he killed. And they chose to forgive him.

So, what's the point? Simply this: The only one who is in a position to *not forgive you,* is God. And not only does he *forgive* you, but he also has placed you on his "team"! And as Paul said, "If God is for us, who can be against us?" (Romans 8:31, NIV)

Your salvation is as secure as God himself. From now on, when you sin, you do break your intimacy with God, but you do not lose your salvation. If you can't *earn* your salvation by anything you do (see chapter 5), then you certainly can't *keep* it

by anything you do either.
But God keeps it *for* you — and that's the best news of all!

Lifeline

My salvation is as secure as God himself.

His Lines

Romans 8:39-40

John 10:27-28

The Bottom Line (For Group Discussion)

1. Even though my behavior doesn't *earn* salvation, is it possible that my behavior can *prove* whether or not I really am a Christian? (*Hint:* The following verses may be helpful in stimulating a discussion: James 2:18-20; 1 Peter 2:12; John 13:14-15.)

2. Do you know any "Lone Ranger Christians," who think they don't need to hang around other Christians? Are they right in thinking that way?

3. Using the motif of food, have the members of the group discuss what other forms of food they feed themselves throughout the week. (i.e. music, media, etc.) Is it junk food, or nutritious?

4. Survey the members of the group, and see if they would be interested in continuing to meet as a group and study *Some Assembly Required* together. If so, arrange a time to begin meeting.

Bible Verses Referred to in This Book

Chapter 1
Genesis 1:26-27 Then God said, "Let us make a man — someone like ourselves, to be the master of all life upon the earth and in the skies and in the seas." So God made man like his Maker. Like God did God make man; Man and maid did he make them.

Genesis 5:1 Here is a list of some of the descendants of Adam — the man who was like God from the day of his creation.

Genesis 9:6 Any man who murders shall be killed; for to kill a man is to kill one made like God.

Jeremiah 9:24 Let them boast in this alone: That they truly know me, and understand that I am the Lord of justice and of righteousness whose love is steadfast; and that I love to be this way.

Jeremiah 31:3 For long ago the Lord had said to Israel: I have loved you, O my people, with an everlasting love; with lovingkindness I have drawn you to me.

Jeremiah 31:34 At that time it will no longer be necessary to admonish one another to know the Lord. For everyone, both great and small, shall really know me then, says the Lord, and I will forgive and forget their sins.

John 3:16 For God loved the world so much that he gave his only Son so that anyone who believes in him shall not perish but have eternal life.

John 17:3 And this is the way to have eternal life — by knowing you, the only true God, and Jesus Christ, the one you sent to earth!

Chapter 2
Genesis 2:15-17 The Lord God placed the man in the Garden of Eden as its gardener, to tend and care for it. But the Lord God gave the man this warning: "You may eat any fruit in the garden except fruit from the Tree of Conscience — for its fruit will open

your eyes to make you aware of right and wrong, good and bad. If you eat its fruit, you will be doomed to die."

Genesis 3:1-7 The serpent was the craftiest of all the creatures the Lord God had made. So the serpent came to the woman. "Really?" he asked. *"None* of the fruit in the garden? God says you mustn't eat *any* of it?" "Of course we may eat it," the woman told him. "It's only the fruit from the tree at the *center* of the garden that we are not to eat. God says we mustn't eat it or even touch it, or we will die." "That's a lie!" the serpent hissed. "You'll not die! God knows very well that the instant you eat it you will become like him, for your eyes will be opened — you will be able to distinguish good from evil!" The woman was convinced. How lovely and fresh looking it was! And it would make her so wise! So she ate some of the fruit and gave some to her husband, and he ate it too. And as they ate it, suddenly they became aware of their nakedness, and were embarrassed. So they strung fig leaves together to cover themselves around the hips.

Hebrews 9:27 It is destined that men die only once, and after that comes judgment.

Isaiah 59:1-2 Listen now! The Lord isn't too weak to save you. And he isn't getting deaf! He can hear you when you call! But the trouble is that your sins have cut you off from God. Because of sin he has turned his face away from you and will not listen anymore.

James 4:1-2 What is causing the quarrels and fights among you? Isn't it because there is a whole army of evil desires within you? You want what you don't have, so you kill to get it. You long for what others have, and can't afford it, so you start a fight to take it away from them. And yet the reason you don't have what you want is that you don't ask God for it.

Psalm 53:3 But all have turned their backs on him; they are filthy with sin — corrupt and rotten through and through. Not one is good, not one!

Romans 5:12 When Adam sinned, sin entered the entire human race. His sin spread death throughout all the world, so everything began to grow old and die, for all sinned.

Romans 6:23 For the wages of sin is death, but the free gift of God is eternal life through Jesus Christ our Lord.

Romans 7:14-20 The law is good, then, and the trouble is not there but with *me,* because I am sold into slavery with Sin as my owner. I don't understand myself at all, for I really want to do what is right, but I can't. I do what I don't want to — what I hate. I know perfectly well that what I am doing is wrong, and my bad conscience proves that I agree with these laws I am breaking. But I can't help myself, because I'm no longer doing it. It is sin inside me that is stronger than I am that makes me do these evil things. I know I am rotten through and through so far as my old sinful nature is concerned. No matter which way I turn I can't make myself do right. I want to but I can't. When I want to do good, I don't; and when I try not to do wrong, I do it anyway. Now if I am doing what I don't want to, it is plain where the trouble is: sin still has me in its evil grasp.

Chapter 3

Ephesians 2:8-9 Because of his kindness you have been saved through trusting Christ. And even trusting is not of yourselves; it too is a gift from God. Salvation is not a reward for the good we have done, so none of us can take any credit for it.

John 5:39-40 "You search the Scriptures, for you believe they give you eternal life. And the Scriptures point to me! Yet you won't come to me so that I can give you this life eternal!"

Matthew 7:22-23 "At the Judgment many will tell me, 'Lord, Lord, we told others about you and used your name to cast out demons and to do many other great miracles.' But I will reply, 'You have never been mine. Go away, for your deeds are evil.'"

Psalm 11:7 For the Lord is righteous, he loves justice; upright men will see his face. *(New International Version)*

Romans 3:10 As it is written: "There is no one righteous, not even one." *(New International Version)*

Romans 3:20 Therefore no one will be declared righteous in his sight by observing the law; rather, through the law we become conscious of sin. *(New International Version)*

Chapter 4

2 Corinthians 5:21 For God took the sinless Christ and poured into him our sins. Then, in exchange, he poured God's goodness into us!

John 1:29 The next day John saw Jesus coming toward him and said, "Look! There is the Lamb of God who takes away the world's sin!"

Matthew 9:13 Then he added, "Now go away and learn the meaning of this verse of Scripture, 'It isn't your sacrifices and your gifts I want — I want you to be merciful.' For I have come to urge sinners, not the self-righteous, back to God."

1 Peter 3:18 Christ also suffered. He died once for the sins of all us guilty sinners, although he himself was innocent of any sin at any time, that he might bring us safely home to God. But though his body died, his spirit lived on.

Romans 5:6 When we were utterly helpless with no way of escape, Christ came at just the right time and died for us sinners who had no use for him.

Romans 5:8 But God showed his great love for us by sending Christ to die for us while we were still sinners.

1 Timothy 1:15-16 How true it is, and how I long that everyone should know it, that Christ Jesus came into the world to save sinners — and I was the greatest of them all. But God had mercy on me so that Christ Jesus could use me as an example to show everyone how patient he is with even the worst sinners, so that others will realize that they, too, can have everlasting life.

1 Timothy 2:3-6a This is good and pleases God our Savior, for he longs for all to be saved and to understand this truth: *That God is on one side and all the people on the other side, and Christ Jesus,* *himself man, is between them to bring them together, by giving his life for all mankind.*

Chapter 5

Ephesians 2:8 Because of his kindness you have been saved through trusting Christ. And even trusting is not of yourselves; it too is a gift from God.

Ephesians 3:17 And I pray that Christ will be more and more at home in your hearts, living within you as you trust in him. May your roots go down deep into the soil of God's marvelous love.

Galatians 2:20 I have been crucified with Christ: and I myself no longer live, but Christ lives in me. And the real life I now have within this body is a result of my trusting in the Son of God, who loved me and gave himself for me.

John 5:24 "I say emphatically that anyone who listens to my message and believes in God who sent me has eternal life, and will never be damned for his sins, but has already passed out of death into life."

1 John 5:11-12 And what is is that God has said? That he has given us eternal life, and that this life is in his Son. So whoever has God's Son has life; whoever does not have his Son, does not have life.

Proverbs 4:23 *Above all else, guard your affections.* For they influence everything else in your life.

Romans 6:23 For the wages of sin is death, but the free gift of God is eternal life through Jesus Christ our Lord.

Chapter 6

Galatians 6:2 Share each other's troubles and problems, and so obey our Lord's command.

James 2:18-20 But someone may well argue, "You say the way to God is by faith alone, plus nothing; well, I say that good works are important too, for without good works you can't prove whether you have faith or not; but anyone can see that I have faith by the way I act." Are there still some among you who hold that "only believing" is enough? Believing in one God? Well, remember that the demons believe this too — so strongly that they tremble in terror! Fool! When will you ever learn that "believing" is useless without *doing* what God wants you to? Faith that does not result in good deeds is not real faith.

John 3:18 "There is no eternal doom awaiting those who trust him to save them. But those who don't trust him have already been tried and condemned for not believing in the only Son of God."

John 5:24 "I say emphatically that anyone who listens to my message and believes in God who sent me has eternal life, and will never be damned for his sins, but has already passed out of death into life."

John 10:27-29 "My sheep recognize my voice, and I know them, and they follow me. I give them eternal life and they shall never perish. No one shall snatch them away from me, for my Father has given them to me, and he is more powerful than anyone else, so no one can kidnap them from me."

John 13:14-15 And since I, the Lord and Teacher, have washed your feet, you ought to wash each other's feet. I have given you an example to follow: do as I have done to you.

1 John 1:9 But if we confess our sins to him, he can be depended on to forgive us and to cleanse us from every wrong. [And it is perfectly proper for God to do this for us because Christ died to wash away our sins.]

1 John 3:19-20 Then we will know for sure, by our actions, that we are on God's side, and our consciences will be clear, even when we stand before the Lord. But if we have bad consciences and feel that we have done wrong, the Lord will surely feel it even more, for he knows everything we do.

1 Peter 2:12 Be careful how you behave among your unsaved neighbors; for then, even if they are suspicious of you and talk against you, they will end up praising God for your good works when Christ returns.

Proverbs 28:13 A man who refuses to admit his mistakes can never be successful. But if he confesses and forsakes them, he gets another chance.

Romans 8:1 So there is now no condemnation awaiting those who belong to Christ Jesus.

Romans 8:31 What can we ever say to such wonderful things as these? If God is on our side, who can ever be against us?

Romans 8:33 Who dares accuse us whom God has chosen for his own? Will God? No! He is the one who has forgiven us and given us right standing with himself.

Romans 8:34 Who then will condemn us? Will Christ? *No!* For he is the one who died for us and came back to life again for us and is sitting at the place of highest honor next to God, pleading for us there in heaven.

Romans 8:38b-40 Our fears for today, our worries about tomorrow, or where we are — high above the sky, or in the deepest ocean — nothing will ever be able to separate us from the love of God demonstrated by our Lord Jesus Christ when he died for us.

Steps to Peace With God

STEP 1
GOD'S PURPOSE: PEACE AND LIFE

God loves you and wants you to experience peace and life — abundant and eternal.

The Bible says...

"...we have peace with God through our Lord Jesus Christ." Romans 5:1

"For God so loved the world that He gave His only begotten Son, that whoever believes in Him should not perish but have everlasting life." John 3:16

"...I have come that they may have life, and that they may have it more abundantly." John 10:10b

Since God planned for us to have peace and abundant life right now, why are most people not having this experience?

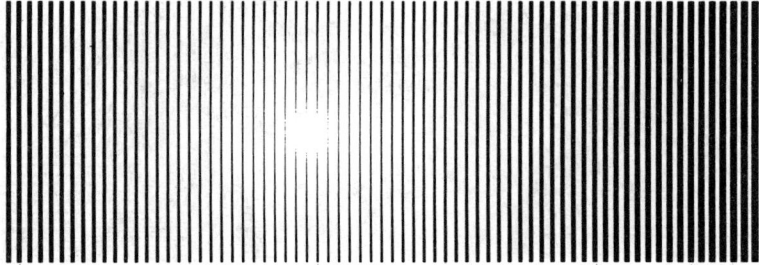

STEP 2

OUR PROBLEM: SEPARATION

God created us in His own image to have an abundant life. He did not make us as robots to automatically love and obey Him, but gave us a will and freedom of choice.

We chose to disobey God and go our own willful way. We still make this choice today. This results in separation from God.

The Bible says... "For all have sinned and fall short of the glory of God." Romans 3:23

"For the wages of sin is death, but the gift of God is eternal life in Christ Jesus our Lord." Romans 6:23

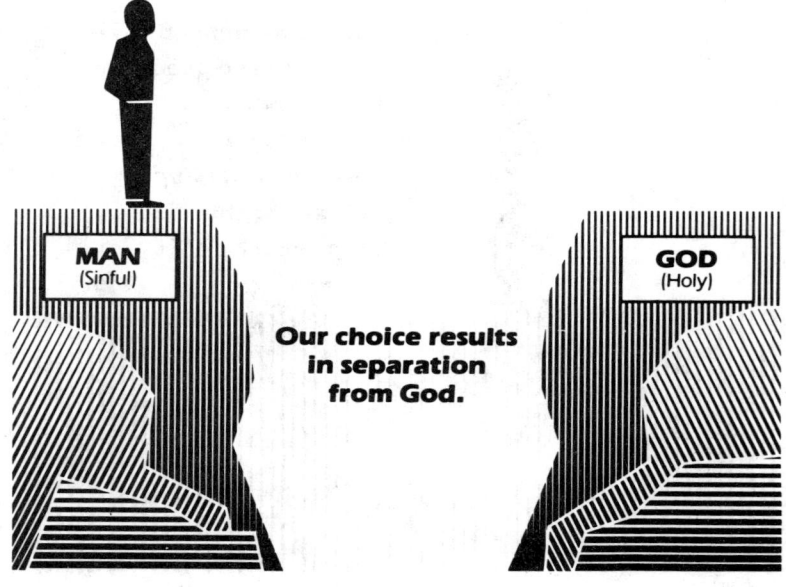

MAN (Sinful)

GOD (Holy)

Our choice results in separation from God.

Our attempts...

Through the ages, individuals have tried in many ways to bridge this gap...without success...

The Bible says...

"There is a way that seems right to a man, but in the end it leads to death." Proverbs 14:12

"But your iniquities have separated you from God; and your sins have hidden His face from you, so that He will not hear." Isaiah 59:2

There is only one remedy for this problem of separation.

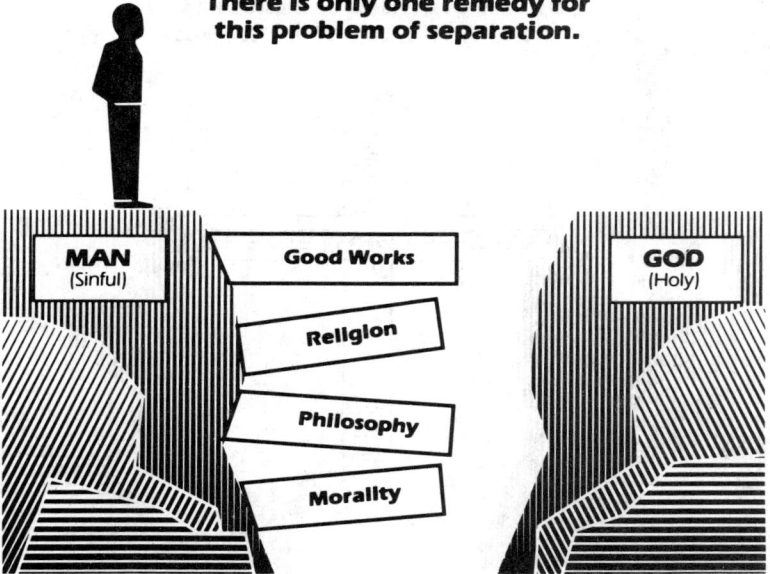

STEP 3

GOD'S REMEDY: THE CROSS

Jesus Christ is the only answer to this problem. He died on the Cross and rose from the grave, paying the penalty for our sin and bridging the gap between God and man.

The Bible says...

"...God is on one side and all the people on the other side, and Christ Jesus, Himself man, is between them to bring them together..." 1 Timothy 2:5

"For Christ also has suffered once for sins, the just for the unjust, that He might bring us to God..." 1 Peter 3:18a

"But God demonstrates His own love for us in this: While we were still sinners, Christ died for us." Romans 5:8

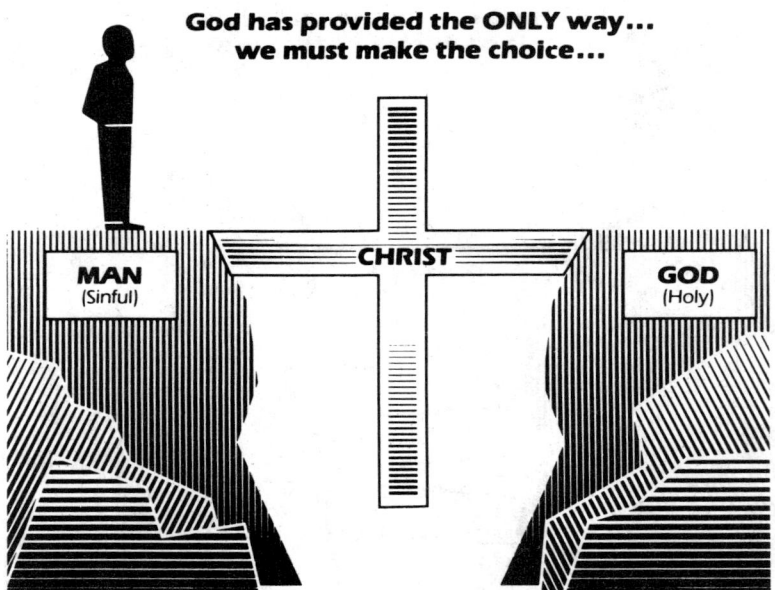

God has provided the ONLY way... we must make the choice...

MAN (Sinful) — CHRIST — GOD (Holy)

STEP 4

OUR RESPONSE: RECEIVE CHRIST

We must trust Jesus Christ and receive Him by personal invitation.

The Bible says...

"Behold, I stand at the door and knock. If anyone hears My voice and opens the door, I will come in to him and dine with him, and he with Me." Revelation 3:20

"But as many as received Him, to them He gave the right to become children of God, even to those who believe in His name." John 1:12

"...If you confess with your mouth the Lord Jesus and believe in your heart that God has raised Him from the dead, you will be saved." Romans 10:9

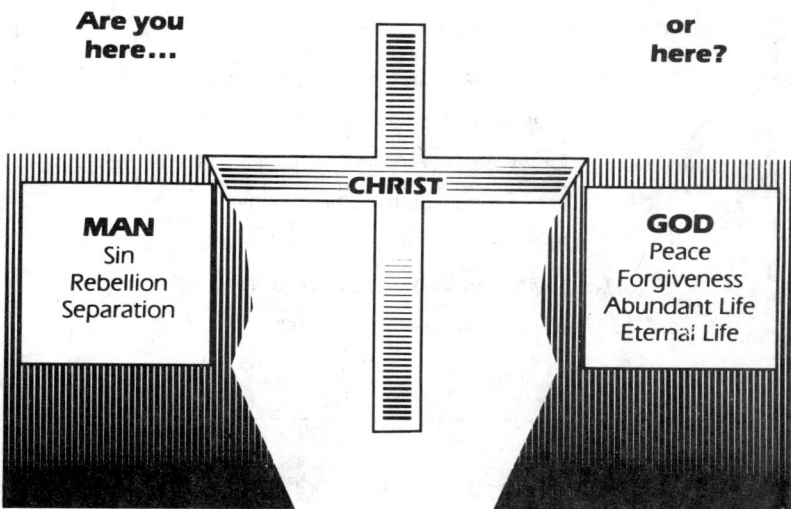

Is there any good reason why you cannot receive Jesus Christ right now?

How to receive Christ:

1. Admit your need (I am a sinner).
2. Be willing to turn from your sins (repent).
3. Believe that Jesus Christ died for you on the Cross and rose from the grave.
4. Through prayer, invite Jesus Christ to come in and control your life through the Holy Spirit. (Receive Him as Lord and Savior.)

WHAT TO PRAY:

Dear Lord Jesus,

I know that I am a sinner and need Your forgiveness. I believe that You died for my sins. I want to turn from my sins. I now invite You to come into my heart and life. I want to trust You as Savior and follow You as Lord, in the fellowship of Your church.

_____ _____
Date   Signature

GOD'S ASSURANCE: HIS WORD

If you prayed this prayer,

The Bible says... "For 'whoever calls upon the name of the Lord will be saved.'" Romans 10:13

Did you sincerely ask Jesus Christ to come into your life? Where is He right now? What has He given you?

"For it is by grace you have been saved, through faith — and this is not from yourselves, it is the gift of God — not by works, so that no one can boast." Ephesians 2:8,9

The Bible says... "He who has the Son has life; he who does not have the Son of God does not have life. These things I have written to you who believe in the name of the Son of God, that you may know that you have eternal life, and that you may continue to believe in the name of the Son of God." 1 John 5:12-13

Receiving Christ, we are born into God's family through the supernatural work of the Holy Spirit who indwells every believer...this is called regeneration or the "new birth."

If you have followed these steps to peace with God, you have begun a wonderful new life in Christ. To strengthen this relationship you should:

1. Read the Bible daily to learn more about Christ and his will for your life.
2. Talk with God each day, praying about your needs and thanking God for his answers.
3. Tell others about Christ and the new life he offers.
4. Attend a church where you can worship God, fellowship with other Christians, and serve Christ.